All About
COLOUR

All About
COLOUR

by Irene Yates
Illustrated by Jill Newton

🌀 Belitha Press

First published in Great Britain in 1997 by
Belitha Press Limited,
London House, Great Eastern Wharf
Parkgate Road, London SW11 4NQ

Series editor: Maria O'Neill
Series designer: Hayley Cove

ISBN 1 85561 563 0

Printed in Portugal.

British Library Cataloguing
in Publication Data
for this book is available
from the British Library.

Contents

What is colour?

Colour is all around us. We find colour everywhere we look. Which colour do you like best?

This is a colour wheel. The six colours in the colour wheel are red, orange, yellow, green, blue and purple.

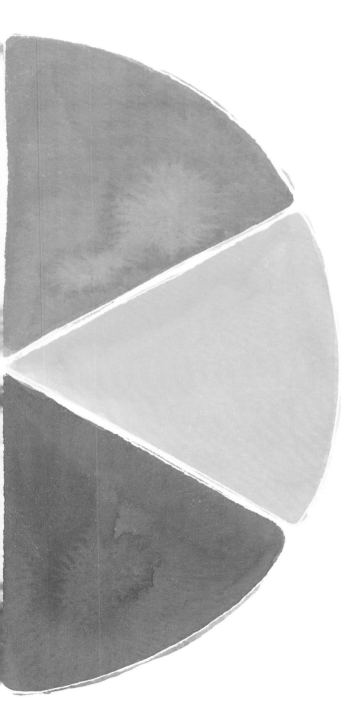

Our world is full of colour. Try to imagine what it would look like if there was no colour.

Here is some bright and colourful fruit.

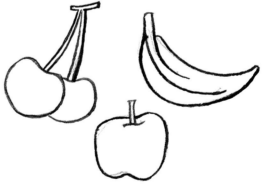

This fruit has no colour. Which fruit looks good to eat?

Making colours

Red, blue and yellow are primary colours. We mix primary colours to make all the other colours.

+ =

+ =

Light and dark colours

You can make colours lighter or darker by adding black or white paint to them.

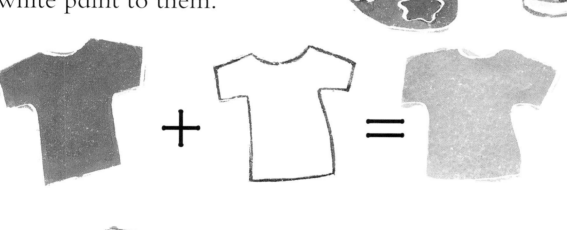

Red

Red is a primary colour. It cannot be made by mixing other colours.

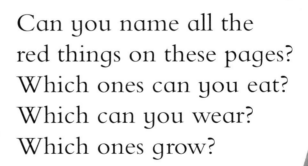

Can you name all the red things on these pages? Which ones can you eat? Which can you wear? Which ones grow?

Red warns of danger. People know there is danger if they see a red sign.

 The ladybird's wings are red and black to warn other creatures not to eat them.

Red means stop.

Make a red collection

Make a collection of lots of different red things. Choose bits of paper, fruit, flowers, vegetables and even clothes.

Blue

Blue is the colour of the sky on a sunny day. Blue is a primary colour.

How many blue things can you see here? Can you find the lightest blue on these pages?

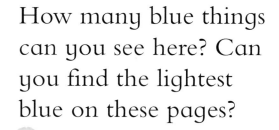

Make new colours

Find some see-through sweet wrappers or plastic bottles that are different colours. Look at blue things through the different colours.

Look among your clothes for blue things. Are any of them the same shade of blue?

Some people have beautiful blue eyes.

A peacock has blue and green coloured feathers.

Yellow

Yellow is a primary colour. Yellow is the colour of lemons and buttercups.

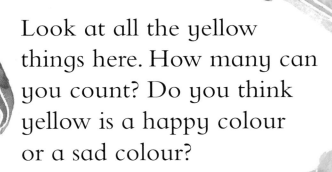

Look at all the yellow things here. How many can you count? Do you think yellow is a happy colour or a sad colour?

The yellow and black stripes of a wasp are very bright. They say 'Beware! The wasp stings'.

If you break an egg, you can see its yellow yolk.

Make yellow shapes

Use crayons to draw a yellow exploding shape. Now draw a yellow peaceful shape. Which does yellow work best for?

The taxis in New York are yellow so they are easy to see in traffic.

Green

Green is the colour of grass. If you mix blue and yellow paint you will see green.

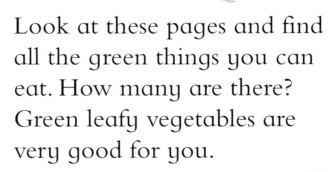

Look at these pages and find all the green things you can eat. How many are there? Green leafy vegetables are very good for you.

This fruit is a plantain. It looks like a banana but it is green.

Grow cress
Sprinkle mustard and cress seeds on some tissue. Keep the seeds moist but do not water them too much. Watch the cress grow in just a few days.

At the traffic lights, green means go.

A greenhouse is built from glass. Inside the greenhouse, plants are warm and sheltered.

Orange

**Orange is a mixture
of red and yellow.
It is a warm colour.**

How many orange things
can you count on this
page? Which of your
toys has an orange part?

Make an orange drink

Squeeze three oranges to
make some orange juice.
Put your orange drink in
the fridge to keep it cool.

A basketball
is orange.
Can you
bounce a ball five
times without stopping?

What does
the amber
light tell
you to do?

Ginger cats are always
male cats. They are
called ginger toms.

Brown

Brown is a natural colour. Brown is the colour of earth and wood.

Can you name all the brown animals on these pages?

Some people have beautiful brown eyes.

Coffee beans grow on small trees. The beans are roasted and ground to make a hot tasty drink.

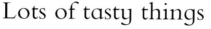

Lots of tasty things to eat are brown. Can you think of any more?

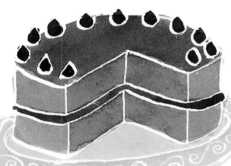

A brown walk

Go for a brown walk. Make a list of all the brown insects, birds, trees and other brown things you see. Find brown leaves, plants, stones and shells.

Purple

Purple is a rich colour. If you mix red and blue paint, you will see purple.

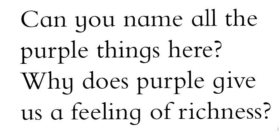

Can you name all the purple things here? Why does purple give us a feeling of richness?

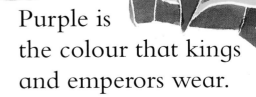

Purple is the colour that kings and emperors wear.

This butterfly has beautiful purple wings.

Paint the king's clothes

Paint a group of kings in new clothes. Paint each king in a different colour. Which king looks the most important?

You can spread blackcurrant jam on a slice of bread.

White

White is a cold colour. White is the colour of snow and ice.

Look at all the white things here. The apples are green on the outside but white on the inside. What else is white inside?

Write your name

Use different coloured chalks to write your name on a chalkboard. Why is white chalk easy to read?

An igloo is a house made of ice.

Snow lies on the ground in a thick blanket. It feels good to be the first person who walks on it.

When the wind blows across the sea the tops of the waves look white.

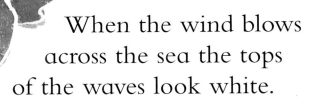

Black

Black is a dark colour. Black is the colour of the sky at night.

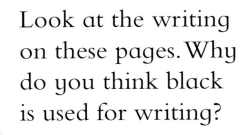

Look at the writing on these pages. Why do you think black is used for writing?

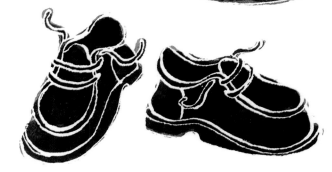

Make your own shadow

Shine a torch against a wall. Make the room dark. Stand in front of the torch and look at your shadow on the wall.

On a sunny day you can see lots of black shadows.

Black grapes are sweet and juicy.

Penguins are shiny black and white birds. They cannot fly but they are good swimmers.

Explore colour

Make a spinning top

1 Cut out a card circle.
2 Paint parts of the circle in different colours.
3 Poke a pencil through the centre to make a top.
4 Spin the top. What happens to the colours?
5 Make more spinning tops using different colours.

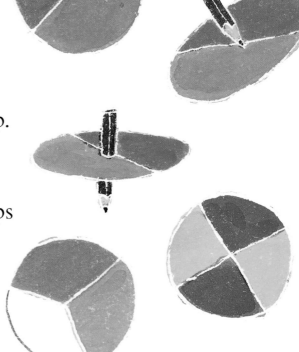

Colouring boats

Draw some boats. How many different ways can you colour the boats using only three colours?

Memory game

Look at the pictures on
this page for one minute.
Cover them up. How many
things can you remember?
Which colours are easy
to remember?

Picture list

Here is a list of all the pictures in this book.

Red Cherries, tomatoes, red hot chillies, tomato sauce, poppy, T-shirt, red pepper, warning sign, traffic lights, ladybirds, wellingtons, strawberry.

Blue Toy brick, blue bird, blue jeans, crayon, bluebells, blue whale, sea, bluebottle, stripy T-shirt, peacock, blue eyes.

Yellow Sun, buttercups, mustard, skateboard, rain hat, lemon, chick, wasp, cheese, egg, daffodils, New York taxi.

Green Peas, apple, sports shirt, umbrella, broccoli, caterpillars, plantain, parrot, traffic lights, greenhouse, green turtle.

Orange Crab, pumpkin, leaf, carrot, goldfish, orange, toy digger, orange juice, basketball, traffic lights, ginger tom cat, leaf.

Brown Violin, tree, nuts, bear, mouse, brown eyes, hare, coffee, weasel, chocolate, chocolate cake, beefburger, boots.

Purple Aubergine, fuschia, scarf, gloves, amethyst ring, emperor, amethyst, butterfly, rucksack, bicycle, blackcurrant jam, violets, plums.

White Snowman, apple, bread, toothpaste, onion, polar bear, snowdrop, igloo, footprints in the snow, duck, glass of milk, waves.

Black Night sky, tyre, black pencil, paint brush and paint, ink, newspaper, shoes, shadow, torch, black grapes, penguin, flippers.

Words to remember

amber an orange colour. On traffic lights it means 'get ready to go'.

amethyst a purple stone used to make jewellery.

aubergine a purple vegetable.

danger a chance of being hurt or harmed.

emperor a ruler, like a king.

exploding bursting with lots of noise and energy.

peaceful quiet and calm.

primary colours red, yellow and blue are primary colours. They are mixed to make other colours.

traffic lights sets of lights which tell the traffic when to stop and when to go.